THE SILENT HOWL

WOLFIA

Clever Fox Publishing
Chennai • Bangalore

CLEVER FOX PUBLISHING
Chennai, India

Published by CLEVER FOX PUBLISHING 2025

ISBN: 978-93-7500-087-7

Dedication:

For the introverted girl-

by nature, or by life

whose young eyes have seen too much

whose tender heart has felt deeply

till she was numb and scarred

this is for you.

It's your space to howl.

CONTENTS

SECTION 1

PERFECTIONS THEY MANIPULATED

ACNE

There lies her acne on her cheeks,
Like thorns on roses that she needs.
People hate acne, that's true,
But who thought it would make her so blue.
The way she goes silent from so loud,
When people point her acne out.
Little does she knows they enhances her beauty,
Like stars accompanying night sky as it's their duty.
There lies her acne on her cheeks,
Like fairy dust a fairy needs.

FLAT IS'NT FAILURE

they talked about my flat chest
their words unkind
judged my body
as if that's how my worth is defined
that time I realized how toxic society could be
their voices spoke a language that was meant to
unshape me
every flower bloom in its season
some late some soon
a shame they covered up with blame
cause they couldn't see beauty in my quite bosom
they said flat meant failure
I said flat meant not falling
for standards soaked in shame
laced with false glory

so much opinion about a body that's not their own
fit unrealistic standards to be known
only when the world finally sees
will it stop selling femininity in silhouettes
for its worth more than mirrors see
while others grew curves, I grew rebellion.
I grew confidence worth more

Then a curve carried on my chest.
I carry mine like a shield-
Not lacking, but lasting.
I protect my heart in solid silence,
A declaration of self-love
And a war
Against what they say a women should be.

OUT CAST OF DESTINY

The world was never hers to begin with-
never her place to stay.
they called her outcast:
outcast of destiny,
outcast of life.
she was a torchlight lit
in a world that never knew night.

They looked at her with pity.
as if she was a flaw meant to be fixed.
being misunderstood became her personality,
a melody mistook for background noise.
the world hurried to label her with names:
shy, silent, pretty, tame.

she dressed in modesty,
always seen in all black.
thought her heart held colors worthy of canvas.
she was a diamond they mistook for mine,
a poetry book they try to define in line.
she was a cosmos mistook for void,
a supernova yet to be deployed.
she made peace with being an outcast,

she never minded not fitting in.
she lived between pages of books,
in the worlds she painted,
in the melodies she hummed,
under the moon's quiet gaze.
she was hauntingly beautiful-
like an abandoned castle.
she lived in all the places
they never dared to dream of.

PATTERNS OF ME

Her skin held patches-
patterns she was ashamed of,
patterns she couldn't erase off.
in shame tears she shed,
a flaw she wished had gone unsaid.

in the shape of patterns
she saw a burn, a stain.
turned back from mirrors,
bled in pain,
bled in shame.

but her skin held marks
of how she was made-
a symbol of love
that would never fade.

A love between
the sun and the moon,
the result of which:
a flower she bloomed.

only if she knew
how her patterns were made,
would she still wish
they would fade?

once, the sun hugged the moon
and left behind a tender trace-
a symbol of love, they made.

her skin held proof of that love,
painted in melanin-
an ancient, sacred bond
she carries.

Now she traces her fingers
on the map of her skin,
a love that still lingers,
as it always has been.

her patterns-
a story of love
the universe created.
living on her skin,
they were fated.

MIRROR, MIRROR

mirror, mirror on the wall,
tell me-why is it me of all?
Tell me why can't I meet my gaze?
Tell me why must I suffer with this face?

Tell me why I got to be the one,
seen by many,
but loved by none.

oh, mirror-
the face I see
is a truth I'm scared to be.

tell me, mirror,
who do I blame
for this map of flaws
marked in shame?

Only if I could close my eyes,
be somewhere
away from this sight.

With sincerity, the mirror replies:
oh! sweetheart, look me in the eyes.
lift your face, meet your gaze,
and see the delight that's your face.

Lift your hand and trace your lines-
see the beauty that's divine.
oh! sweetheart, you're the one
that people dream of under the sun.

The face you see is a truth you wear,
the kind of beauty that's seen rare.
Only if from my eyes you could see,
you would know how you're a blessing to be.

CONSTELLATION OF ME

freckles I have all over my face-
shameful dots marking my skin.
a dot so tiny,
but its shame so bright.
freckles I tried to cover and hide.

they dulled my beauty,
covered my shine.
freckles I could never call mine.

people said to cover up-
it's a flaw meant to be gone.
they called it a blemish...
but were they all wrong?

for I never called it a flaw
before they did.
tiny stars,
I never really wanted hid.

my freckles aren't imperfection,
but stars aligned.

each holds a beauty-
unique, divine.

constellation of stardust
beneath my eyes,
a resemblance to stars
across the skies.

constellation of stories
marked on my skin-
stories of me
from deep within.

ROOTS OF ME

Their hair—
silken threads that flow,
in soft winds
they gently blow.
Hair so pretty,
every strand fine—
I envy all hair
that isn't mine.
A crown of sorrows
on my head,
unworthy of
each tear I shed.
But as time passed,
the conflict faded.
These roots are mine—
a part of how I'm made.

My strands,
wild and free,
capture the journey
to finally be me.
They hold memories—
good and bad,

hugged me gently
whenever I was sad.
How can I not love them?
They've been with me
in my low and prime.
When others turned away,
they stood strong and tall—
held me together
through every fall.
They aren't just hair,
but memories
woven in thread—
a crown I now carry,
proudly knit
on my head.

NATURE'S FRAGMENTS

Doesn't the moon have scars to feel shame?
Yet wolfling you love it just the same.
It doesn't hide behind clouds or beg for light-
It glows with every wound, every fight.
Yes, the perfection may seem pretty, a dreamy sight
But why don't you see the beauty in darkness
and stop chasing the light?
The Earth's uneven, it's reign terrain
but don't we love the feel of it in our feet, wet with
rain?
You try to sculpt your face, your body and figure to
stand tall,
But would you do the same with your childhood's
favorite doll?
You think Nature's imperfections are itself a pretty
view,
Why can't you
think the same for someone you always knew?

SECTION 2

THE WEIGHT OF SILENCE

BALCONY THOUGHTS

I entered my balcony
to be greeted by an empty dark sky.
Sat beside a weed
growing from a crack—
unwanted and unchecked.
That's the best nature could have explained me.
Staring at the streets endlessly,
wondering what the world has done to me.
Sure, I was never talkative—
but my thoughts have silenced too.
Always careful not to hurt others,
forgetting I could be hurt too.
A lot has died inside of me.
Only a body with a soul remains.
Would I retreat to heaven like this—
as a life that went in vain?

GHOST TOWN

As I walk through these silent streets, they are a mess
of dirt,
fallen signboards that could no longer stand strong,
as if navigating these lands was a pride way longer
gone.
The stillness lingers as if silent voices calling out.
Footfalls linger, laughter echoes, shadows stretch as
the night falls,
as if the patterns were memorized by the walls.
Each corner holds a story, a memory now buried in
silence,
yet its presence couldn't be silenced.
The streets that once held not just houses but homes,
not just busy markets but connections that felt whole.
Now the buildings collapsed, markets died,
now the town is left with nothing to hide.
The world forgets, the wind remembers passing by
still,
the routines, the people, the pattern as it wills.
The park that was alive with children's light,
now waiting, abandoned, dead in sight.
The stories, the memories, the tales it holds,
now a painful memory better left untold.

The doors of the house crack open as if inviting you
in,
to tell a story of an old friend, how their life here's
been.
The living room wasn't living anymore,
no one dined at the dining table,
the shared bedrooms were mutually abandoned.
The walls held photo frames with shattered glass,
as if the glass refused to frame memories of those who
abandoned it,
yet it can't quite pierce the photo away.
People's favorite restaurant also called "The Gathering
Spot"
was now struggling to gather what was left.
The town's tourist spot known as "The Pride of Town"
was now shamefully dead.
An empty canvas, yet strangely whole.
The whispered past still lingers in its soul.
The cracks on earth lay silent dead
as if they mourned the town's wreath.

As if the town held its breath,
refusing to let go of the little it had.
The passerby looks at the town with their pitiful gaze,
yet it was always unworthy of their days.
A place where memories used to stay,
a heart it is what they say.

THE 3 AM'S MARE

At night when the clock strikes three
A demon is set free
A demon that haunts my night
The nightmare I could never fight
My eyes open, my body is still
I am caged to my bed against my will
Hands try to choke me down
I tried to scream, but no sound came out
Screaming, crying, demonic groove
A voice in my head repeats—"I can't move, I can't move."

The ceiling stares like it knows my name,
While shadows crawl through my window frame.
I beg for breath, for light, for grace—
But demon hunts and leaves no trace
My tears don't fall, they hover tight,
Like trying to dim the blur of night
I blacked out back into the dark
But this time with night's cruel mark.

DESKBOUND SEED: THE ORIGIN

In solitude, my feelings blown—
A shadow crept, unseen, unknown.
It haunts me down, my heartbeat slow,
A river of tears I let quietly flow.
I hid beneath a fragile sheathe,
But I was suffocating—I couldn't breathe.
As panic fades to trembling sniffs,
I slip into dreams like falling cliffs.
Suddenly, I'm that child again,
At her desk, pretending back then.
Last night's ruin flashes—my hand trembles again.
Anxiety... that's where it all began.

CASTLE OF GLASSES

They stacked expectations crystal thin
Sharp loads pressed on my frozen skin.
Each a fragile, delicate feather—
Careful, calculated—I stacked one on another.
Deadlines, dreams, assignments, classes—
A trembling card castle made of glasses.
Though the threat of collapse loomed tall,
With hope, I held them all.
But how long can a castle stay still,
When life moves against your will?
As my tower struggled to withstand,
I tried to mend it with trembling hands.
Then came what I feared—clear and severe:
The sound of shattering glasses rang in my ear.

ME-YOU-SE

Dusk broke into dawn again.
I looked at the morning sky—I see no end.
The rush I can't beat, every day on repeat,
Walking on shards of glass, bare feet.
I chose this path, now fog blurs my sight.
Every day gets a little harder to fight.
I run in this dark loop, chasing light,
Holding onto feelings perhaps too tight.

Now as the night blooms, I'm under the moon,
Dreaming, perhaps, to be you too soon.
When life gets too hard to get through,
I close my eyes and think of you.

A successful woman, fierce and bold,
She who broke beyond the sky's hold.
A lotus bloomed from the darkest mud,
She who stood through every flood.
She who leads with wisdom and care,
A woman who has nothing to fear.

She who earned the place she stands,
Built from ashes with her hands.
A woman whose eyes hold the sea—
Deep waves, untamed and free.
A woman who loves and respects herself,
Who never needed no one else.
She holds a power that makes empires fold.
Her worth is measured beyond gold.

I'll cross eternity, oceans, and a lot,
To see you be everything I'm not.

SAME SKY, SAME SCARS

I know the lonely balcony nights,
When the thoughts are heavier than silence,
And the city air hums a strange melody.
I have built ghost towns too,
Walk through the lonely streets inside my rib cage.
I have fought 3 AM's monsters too,
That chokes you down and tell you- you are not
enough.
Times when your fears get a strong hold,
Just know this- you are not alone.
Cause even a child with trembling hands,
Can sculpt a world from ashes and sand.
Even when the castle of glasses break,
The dusk clears and new hope awake.
And when you meet your future self-, you'll see,
That she is made of your every trembling plea.
Wolfling, don't you fear the pitch-black night,
A hopeful dawn will break through bright.
Your fears and doubts will set you free,
You'll realize you are everything you wish to be.

SECTION 3
SCARLET SCARS

FADING IT GOES

I no longer remember your eyes,
Or the way you smiled.
Forgetting the moments we never really shared,
Oh! How I wished that you cared.
I don't remember your voice anymore,
Looks like our ship has reached its shore.
Our story was painted in a faded blue,
Like my love, you are fading too.

SAND CASTLE

Sandcastle of memories we built together,
Swearing upon it promises forever.
The waves were gentle, the winds were kind,
Everything was alright till your hand held mine.

Now I cupped our memories in grains of sand,
Memories that are struggling to withstand.
The tighter I hold the more it slips-
Love undone by time's eclipse.

The tide took what I tried to save,
Our story buried beneath its wave.
Maybe it was always meant to fall,
But in the corner of heart a wish still calls.

DO YOU?

I know we are doing fine,
You are with your people; I am with mine.
You look happy, certainly you do,
But do you think this happiness is fleeting, the way I
do.
Do you wish it was still us now,
Like we get back together somehow.
Do you wish we run into each other,
And find a reason to stick together.
Do you still have something left to say,
Do you wish it's enough to make me stay.
Does it hurt when you remember me,
Like part of me is buried in your heart deeply.
Do you smile when you see something I love,
Or push back memories with painful shove.
Does it hurt when she meets your gaze,
Do you remember the way I looked at your face.
How does it feel when you pass by our memories
Streetly,
Do you speed up your pace or breathe in the air
deeply.
Maybe we have healed, maybe it's a lie,
But this love never really dies.

TO LOVE THE RUIN

To love you was to betray myself
I was the girl who never needed help
Yet I looked at you like only you could set me free
Your eyes never softened-not once for me
I traced the way to you so you wouldn't be stray
I painted you in all my colors and you just left me grey
I tried still to carve 'us'
I tried trusting you thought I couldn't trust
You said you couldn't see my tears
Yet you tore me apart
All that's left now is just a broken heart...

ANCIENT ASHES

I see you across the room
When I do I feel something bloom
There's something about your eyes- like I've fell for them before
Like even before the sea was introduced to the shore
A red string pulled between us
Yet not strong enough to seal us
This is something sacred-I feel it through
The way you look at me-I know you do feel it too
Is this delusion or something divine
Now that's a story I dare not define

The moon smiled down, softly weeping light.
The night was cold, the wind mourning their might.
The trees whispered stories the souls never knew,
and the stars blinked slowly, as if grieving too.
The earth held its breath when they passed by—
two hearts stitched by fate, yet cursed to deny.
Nature watched them fight for love they couldn't claim,
and wept for the fire that never became flame.

It began in war, in hateful flames
They were enemies first, then lovers unnamed.
They fought each other before they fought the world,
and when they finally fell, the stars unfurled.
But love was forbidden, and time was cruel.
They held hands through chaos, broke every rule.
Tears carved rivers where their bodies once lay,
and whispered "why's" echoed as they slipped away.
Before losing each other, they made a vow—
There will be a lifetime. Not this. Not now.
But a day will come, when we will finally be one.

CURSED CROWN

The story starts in magic
It ends just tragic
The flower died before its seed was sown
A honey tongued prince to tame me
I'll mess don't blame me
Evil princess doesn't need to be rescued
prince charming didn't remembered her face but the shoe
The beast didn't love the girl just the view
They're loyal till the next girl walks through
Aladin lied his way to royal rim
Talking reindeer Kristoff's only thing
They need therapy not a wedding ring
Eric didn't love her just her sound
Philip kissed her when she was spell bound
Respect's not rocket science it's a rule
These princes need a one-way trip back to school
The prince stumbles, falls off the pages
I burned the story with my rage
I won't play the bird in your golden cage
Keep your kingdom, keep your throne
I'll build my queendom on my own
Alone but love won't chain my bones
Happily, ever after? Sorry not in my poems.

HURT NO MORE

My wolfling your fur is scarred,
I see the places where the hunters have harried.
Your howl has a new lonely sound,
Your soul is wary from your old wounds.
Love is supposed to make you feel whole,
Not something that drains your soul.
I know its hard you are hurt to core,
You have trusted till you can't no more.
But here the pack is different
When you are lost in the cold haze of night
And the echoes of old fears are held tight
Hesitate no longer, take my hand, I've reached out for you
They are warm and will help you see the world a new
Together we will howl under the moon so far
And draw stars around your scars.
Through the journey to find you, I'll walk besides,
So, you could see the light that lives inside
I'll hold you tight till the clouds of doubts are blown
Because you never walk alone.

SECTION 4

THE EERIE DREAM SCAPE

A FEAST OF REGRET

The banquet is set with all my yesterday's,
One that I would fix if I had a way.
A feast I did not ask for and will not be forgiven,
Yet I have to gulp it down for my sins to be even.
The silver platter served rudeness as my starter,
A hard lump down my throat as my arrogance shatter.
The soup burned hot with heat of shame,
For the souls that flinched hearing my name.
I reached for the glass when my throat felt sore,
A bitter tincture of remorse for every cry from my source.
Betrayal arrives as main course with best regards,
I chew it down as splinters and shards.
A special drink prepared for my bout,
I choked on every time I have cursed out.
Desert of selfishness decorated in place,
Bitter metallic taste I savored with disgrace.
I ate my share of course and drank the dreg,
A feast of regret with silent begs.
Nothing can be done, nothing ever would,
I have sinned as much as one could.

A LOVER'S GHOST

The house is quiet, still and wrong,
While I hear faint hum of your favorite song.
My heart is hollow painted in grief,
While you departed like autumn leaf.

I miss the warm embrace of your hug,
My heart pinch at the sight of your coffee mug.
I beg for you in prayers, in dark, in light,
For water as a thirsty might.

The shadows shifted, your presence lingered near,
But your touch is colder that death itself, I fear.
Your face was blank, your lips pale bule,
A ghost returned, but not you I knew.

Your eyes regard me with a strange gleam,
Terrified, I bit back a scream.
I begged you back from heaven,
For you to haunt my dreams.

SEVEN MINUTES

Seven minutes down the memory lane
Each a gentle whisper of pain
Sweet poison poured in seven
Before I begin my journey to heaven

Seven minutes.
Arguments outside the closed door
That left the child on the cold marble floor
Body numbs as the voices clash
Each word hurt sharper than glass

Six minutes.
A teenager with shaking hands
While the young mind registered more than it could withstand
The mirror stares back with a stranger's face
Silent storm raging with no safe space

Five minutes.
In school's backyard their laughter roar
Cause the teen was a loner and nothing more
Their hands were cruel, their gazes cold
Nose was bleeding but what's hurting was soul

Four minutes.
I was suffocating, the room served as cage
So, I followed my emotions led by rage
My hands don't stop till they tear apart
I painted the walls in bloody art

Three minutes.
The world halted when I met your eyes
You smiled with ease, a fox in disguise
My heart was yours in every way
Yet not enough to make you stay

Two minutes.
Our disagreement turned to fight that night
Words like dagger sharp and bright
Our rings sat on the table, cold and still
While a signature closed our story on our will

One minute.
My empire flattered, plans fell like rain
As I watched my dreams go in vain
Years of hard work slipped by
A sigh escape – hope had died

At the reminder – for once memories didn't sting
I let out a sigh and carefully blink
A weak smile broke as I lay still
I ascended to heaven shivering with thrills.

UNINVITED METAMORPHOSIS

It was a tiny thing – a tickle beneath my skin
A shiver ran thick through my vein
My eyes held cold monstrous gaze
At first sight I couldn't recognize my face
My jaw was tight, planes more jut
While the human resemblance slowly shut.

My teeth were replaced with a pair of fangs
While sharp claws switched my hands
My voice grew jagged, rough and foul
While my laugh curled into a beast's growl
Rage burned through my soul and head
I fed while innocent bled.

I feel them watching, their eyes growing fear
As if the scent of monsters has spread in the air
Eyes wide with horror, they froze in place
As shadows of terror consumed their space
I saw the terror on a loved one's face
My human self has vanished without a trace.

THE SIREN'S SONG

The siren's voice calls across the sea
Her song, a spell no sailor can flee
"Come meet your doom, I'll guide your way
Deep into the ocean, your bones will stay
Come meet your doom, I'll sing your heart's desire
While I slowly set your world on my sea fire
Come meet your doom, I'll take you far
Drown you down, till your limbs come apart
Come meet your doom, I'll hush your storm
And burry your soul where dark tides form
Come meet your doom, I'll give you fortune to hold
Take my cursed coin and watch it burry your soul
Come meet your doom – the tide swallowed those
who dared
No voice remained for the tale to be shared
Barter your soul, my trades have price to pay
Careful when you hear me say-"come meet your
doom".

THE DIGITAL GHOST

I blinked and the lens swallowed me whole,
A grin caught in pixels while I am in a scroll.
They laugh at the moments being replay,
I am here terrified but can't look away.

Eyes on screen gazing my face,
I watch them stare, trapped in endless space.
Each moment they shared, my torment unnamed,
A digital ghost forever framed.

THE BEAUTIFUL MESS OF BECOMING

Even when the banquet is set with dismay
A feast of regret as they say
When the lover's ghost haunts you down
And the shared memories linger around.

When the seven minutes comes in painful waves
The weight of memories you can't escape
Let the uninvited metamorphosis come
And feel the unfamiliar music of it hum.

When the siren's song pulls you to seas unknown
Fear not, your doom is something it cannot own
Let the digital ghost hum in the corner of your mind
And let its quite hum eventually bind and unwind.

Yet wolfling broken things can be made new
Be not ashamed of learning you went through
Wear your battle scars like a crown
And let your fire burn the shadows down.

SECTION 5

THE ASHES OF ONCE

THE SMALL FUNERAL

A sorrow blew where her cementation beholds
The atmosphere choked with grief and cold
A small white coffin, a toy placed upon the polished wood
A child mercilessly snatched from her childhood
The sepulchral hush of a forgotten sound
Memories crept through the chapel in rusted bounds.

A florid bouquet curling at the edge with death
Eyes witnessed yet no tear was shed
White lilies wilt in a ring along marigold
Death was a toy too heavy to hold
The world whispered no one was to blame
Yet she bore the silent weight of two names.

I walked near the coffin, this was the coldest spring
Like a bud that never flowered, caterpillar never grew wings
I knelt beside the coffin, feeling it was a dream
I maintained silence though my instincts were to scream
As I lay the roses beside the toys piled
I was attending the funeral of my inner child.

A POET'S TRAGEDY

The ink was black and bled from veins
A grip on pen, the world disdain
She bled on papers, inscribing truth in verse
Create from destruction, a writer's curse
She stitched metaphors till the page was whole
Even exserted she translated her soul.
Color for ink, she traded her youth
And made of teenage a beautiful untruth
With every passing year the writer became gaunt
Till the manuscript was cursed and verses haunt
She lived between pages till reality collide
With a last poetry piece, the writer died.

THE COST TO FEEL

The cold wind blows—my body goes numb.
A strange melody in the night hums.
I wait for minutes, for hours still,
For something—anything—I could feel.

The numbness lingers, eating my soul.
I try to feel, yet I'm empty as whole.
So, I reach for the only way I know:
Cut my skin till the bone shows.

When pain arrives, I remind myself I'm alive.
My lip's part with a painful cry.
But there's pleasure in pain I can't deny.
A cut or two might heal—
Yet there aren't many moments when I feel.

CURSED – LOVE

You held my hand and, in that touch,
You sealed a spell that meant so much
We giggled and made memories of gold
Till your eyes lacked softness and hands grew cold
Your laughter was my favorite sound
Your absence left me hurt and wound.

When did I trust you with my heart
So intense that you broke it apart
Why did you stay when you had to leave
And gifted me a broken bond to grieve
I hate you for what you did
I hate me more for not seeing the betrayal hid.

I feel nothing but apathy when I look at you
You were never the person I thought I knew
You spun stories and call me bitter
When you just hate that without you, I'm better
I cut you off and broke my ties
I am living well without your twisted lies.

DON'T

Little wolfling don't follow my trail,
It's lined with wilted flowers and paper veils.
I buried my own small hands beneath this ground,
A funeral held with no mourning sound.

I wrote myself hollow just to prove I could feel,
Bled words like poison for a love that wasn't real.
Every page cost piece, I'll never regain,
don't trade your heart just to taste pain.

AUTHOR'S NOTE

At first, my poems were never meant to be released. I just wrote whenever I needed to let things out. It's my way of coping things. Yet this time I felt like I needed to do this. My fifteenth year wasn't my best; I had a lot of regrets but it's never too late to do something right? The thought of my poems existing in this world, my voice living on years after I die, thrilled me. But I was hesitant, many times I thought I couldn't make it, but I did. My love for writing made me do it. My work may not be perfect, it was never meant to be. It is my voice and of those who relate to me. It's the beginning of something new with me as Wolfia and my readers as wolflings. I am excited for my new journey ahead; I am open to the praise and criticism if valid.

Thanks to the clever fox publishing team for the guidance and help.

And a special thank you to my older sister (my forever saviour) for always supporting and believing in me, without her this wouldn't be possible.

-wolfia <3

To stay in touch with wolfia

Instagram: https://www.instagram.com/wolfiaverse

Website: https://sites.google.com/view/wolfia/home